THE PAPER AiRPLANE BOOK FOR KiDS

"never give up because great things take time"

this book belongs to

_____

_____

CONTENTS

What makes paper airplanes fly?...................................... 5

Projects... 6

Project templates..48

Disclaimer

This book was made in black and white for lower printing costs and for a cheaper price for our final customers
We hope you enjoy it.

What Makes Paper Airplanes Fly?

Aerodynamics

What makes a paper airplane fly? Air — the stuff that's all around you. Hold your hand in front of your body with your palm facing sideways so that your thumb is on top and your pinkie is facing the floor. Swing your hand back and forth. Do you feel the air? Now turn your palm so it is parallel to the ground and swing it back and forth again, like you're slicing it through the air. You can still feel the air, but your hand is able to move through it more smoothly than when your hand was turned up at a right angle. How easily an airplane moves through the air, or its aerodynamics, is the first consideration in making an airplane fly for a long distance.

Drag and Gravity

Planes that push a lot of air, like your hand did when it was facing the side, are said to have a lot of "drag," or resistance, to moving through the air. If you want your plane to fly as far as possible, you want a plane with as little drag as possible. A second force that planes need to overcome is "gravity." You need to keep your plane's weight to a minimum to help fight against gravity's pull to the ground.

Thrust and Lift

"Thrust" and "lift" are two other forces that help your plane make a long flight. Thrust is the forward movement of the plane. The initial thrust comes from the muscles of the "pilot" as the paper airplane is launched. After this, paper airplanes are really gliders, converting altitude to forward motion. Lift comes when the air below the airplane wing is pushing up harder than the air above it is pushing down. It is this difference in pressure that enables the plane to fly. Pressure can be reduced on a wing's surface by making the air move over it more quickly. The wings of a plane are curved so that the air moves more quickly over the top of the wing, resulting in an upward push, or lift, on the wing.

The Four Forces in Balance

A long flight occurs when these four forces — drag, gravity, thrust, and lift — are balanced. Some planes (like darts) are meant to be thrown with a lot of force. Because darts don't have a lot of drag and lift, they depend on extra thrust to overcome gravity. Long distance fliers are often built with this same design. Planes that are built to spend a long time in the air usually have a lot of lift but little thrust. These planes fly a slow and gentle flight.

ARROW

How it works:

✹ This plane is easy to fold and flies straight and smooth

✹ Add a small amount of up elevator for long level flights.

1.

Orient the template with the "UP" arrow at the top of the page. Then, flip the paper onto its backside, so that you cannot see any of the fold lines.

2.

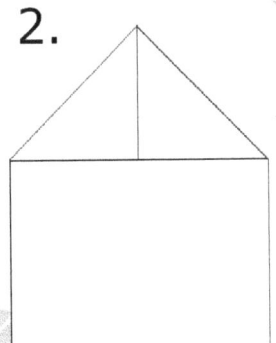

Pull the top right corner down toward you until fold line 1 is visible and crease along the dotted line. Repeat with the top left corner.

3.

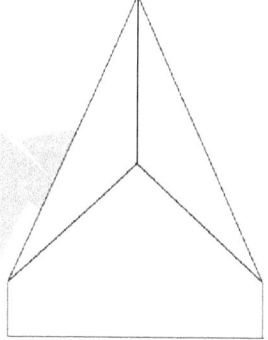

Fold the right side over again and crease along fold line 2. Repeat with the left side.

4.

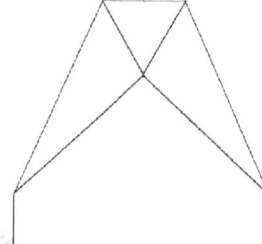

Fold the tip toward you and crease along fold line 3.

ARROW

5.

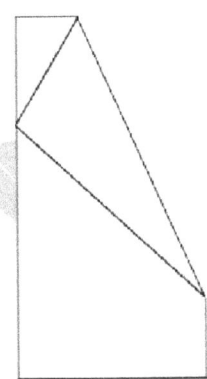

Now, flip the paper over. Then, fold the left side over onto the right side and crease along fold line 4 so that the outside edges of the wings line up.

6.

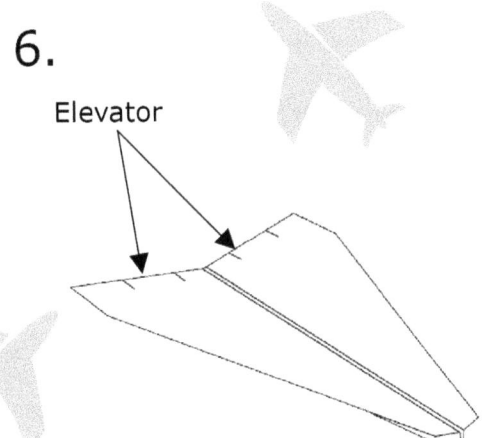

Elevator

Fold the wings down along fold lines 5. Partially open the folds you just created so that the wings stick out straight. Cut two slits, one inch apart, along the back edge of each wing for elevator adjustments. Add wing dihedral by tilting the wings up slightly away from the fuselage. The wings will have a slight "V" shape when viewed from the front. Now we're ready, happy flying!

CANARD

Tips:

★ This plane has small wings at the front called "canards".

★ The design is surprisingly stable and will float long and straight if folded carefully

1.

Orient the template so that the "UP" arrow is at the top of the page. Then flip the paper over so that none of the fold lines are showing.

2.

Fold the top edge of the paper down toward you until fold line 1 becomes visible. Make a crease along the dotted line.

CANARD

3.

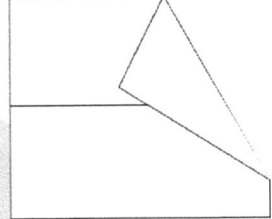

Fold the right corner down and toward you and make a crease along the fold line2. Be aware that you will not be able to see the fold line after making this fold.

4.

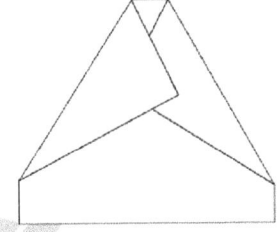

Fold the top left corner down and toward you and make a crease along the fold line 3.

CANARD

5.

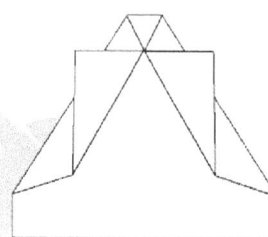

Fold the corners of the flaps you just folded up along fold lines 4.

6.

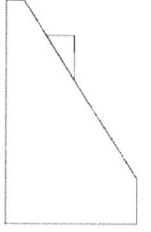

Fold the left half of the plane over onto the right half along fold line 5 so that the outside edges of the wings line up.

CANARD

7.
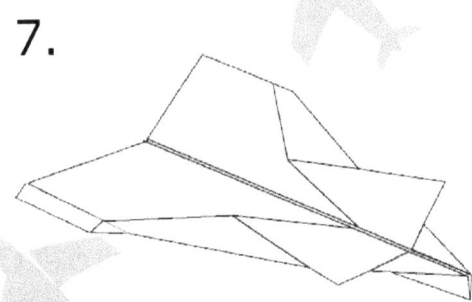

Fold the wings down along fold line 6 and winglets down along fold lines 7. Add wing dihedral by tilting the wings up slightly away from the fuselage. The wings will have a slight "V" shape when viewed from the front.
Happy flying!

CLASSIC DART

Tips:

✸ This plane has short, compact wings and will fly like an arrow

✸ It generally needs some up elevator along the back wing edges to fly properly

1.

Orient the template with the "UP" arrow at the top of the page. Then, flip the paper over onto its backside, so that you cannot see any of the fold lines.

2.

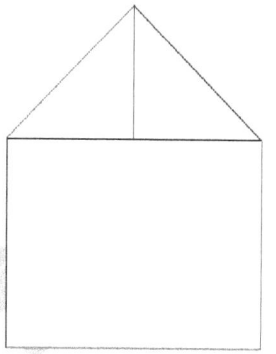

Pull the top right corner down toward you until fold line 1 is visible and crease along the dotted line. Repeat with top left corner.

CLASSIC DART

Tips:

✸ This plane has short, compact wings and will fly like an arrow

✸ It generally needs some up elevator along the back wing edges to fly properly

3.

Fold the top point down toward you until fold line 2 is visible and crease along the dotted line.

4.

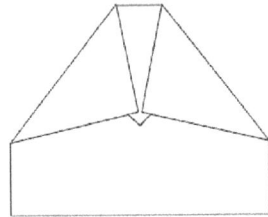

Fold the top left and top right corners down and toward you and crease along fold lines 3.

CLASSIC DART

Tips:

✳ This plane has short, compact wings and will fly like an arrow

✳ It generally needs some up elevator along the back wing edges to fly properly

5.

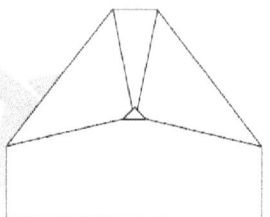

Fold the tip up and over the two diagonal folds along the fold line 4 to secure them in place.

6.

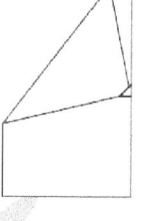

Flip the plane over and fold the right side over onto the left side as shown along fold line 5 so that the outside edges of the wings line up. Also make sure the diagonal folds do not become unstucked from the tip you folded up in the previous step.

CLASSIC DART

Tips:

✸ This plane has short, compact wings and will fly like an arrow

✸ It generally needs some up elevator along the back wing edges to fly properly

7.

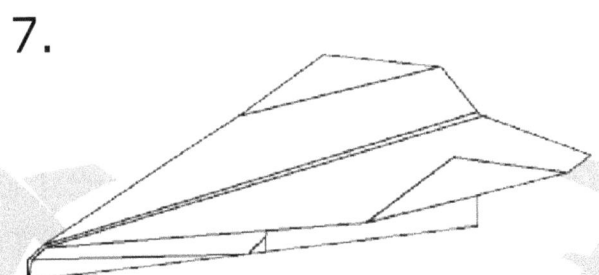

Fold the wings down along the fold lines 6 and the winglets up along fold lines 7. Add wing dihedral by tilting the wings up slightly away from the fuselage. The wings will have a slight "V" shape when viewed from the front. Cut two slits, one inch apart, along the back edge of each wing to make elevator adjustments. Start out by trying some up-elevator.
Happy flying!

CONDOR

How it works:

✹ This plane produces tremendous lift at low speed, giving it a very low glide slope.

✹ It's an excellent indoor flier and will coast across the room on slow, smooth glides.

1.

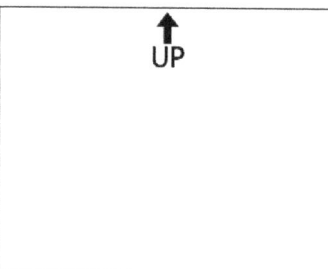

Orient the template with the "UP" arrow a the top of the page. Then, flip the paper over so that none of the fold lines are showing.

2.

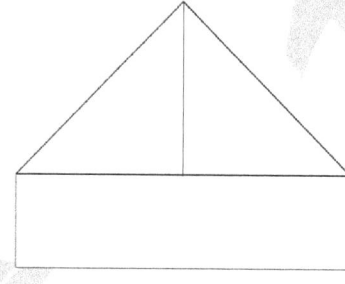

Fold the top left corner down toward you until fold line 1 becomes visible. Crease along the dotted line and repeat with the top right corner.

CONDOR

3.

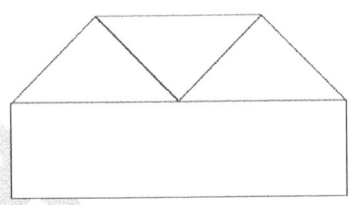

Fold the nose down ultil fold line 2 becomes visible and crease along the dotted line.

4.

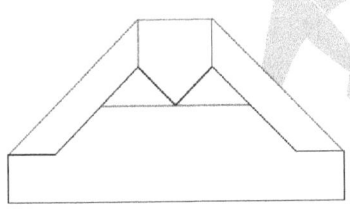

Fold the outside wing edges in and crease along fold lines 3.

CONDOR

5.

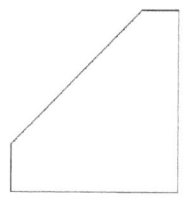

Fold the right half of the plane over the left half and crease along fold line 4 so that the outside edges of the wings line up.

6.

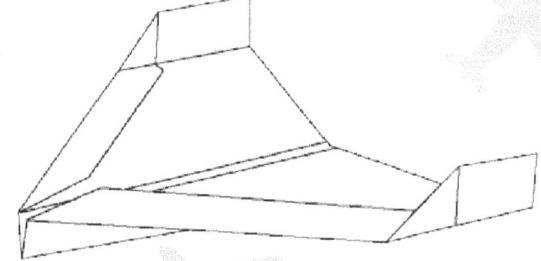

Fold the wings down along fold lines 5 and the winglets up along fold lines 6. Add wing dihedral by tilting the wings up slightly away from the fuselage. The wings will have a slight "V" shape when viewed from the front. Add elevator slits along the back edge of the wings to adjust the flight if necessary. Happy flying!

DELTA

Tips:

✹ This plane fliest fast and straight.

✹ It's easy to fold and a great all around flier. Add some up elevator if necessary to produce stable flights.

1.

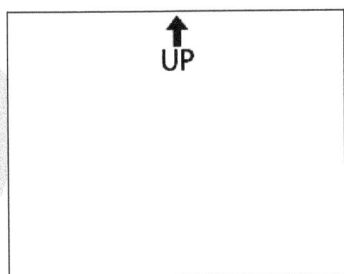

Orient the template so that the "UP" arrow is at the top of the page. Then flip the paper over so that none of the fold lines are showing.

2.

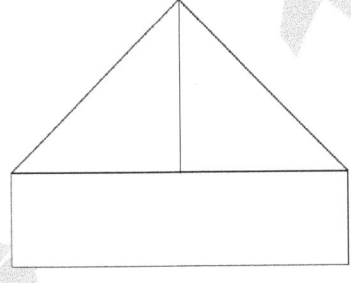

Fold the top left corner down toward you until fold line 1 becomes visible. Crease along the dotted line and repeat with the top right corner.

DELTA

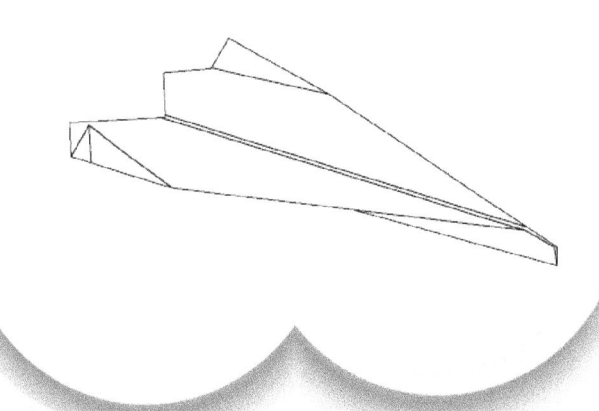

3.

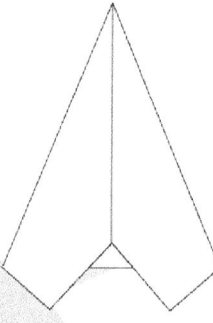

Fold the left side over again and crease along fold line 2. Repeat with the right side.

4.

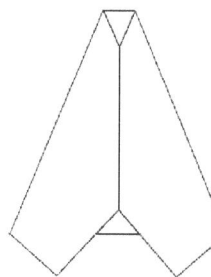

Fold the nose down and toward you along fold line 3.

DELTA

5.

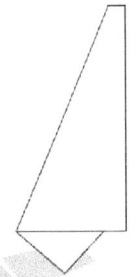

Fold the right half of the plane over the left half along fold line 4 so that the outside edges of the wings line up.

6.

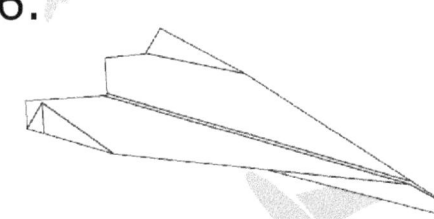

Fold the wings down along fold lines 5 and the winglets up along fold lines 6. Add wing dihedral by tilting the wings up slightly away from the fuselage. The wings will have a slight "V" shape when viewed from the front. Happy flying!

Tips:

✹ This plane is an excellent outdoor glider. Launch straight up and it will glide down in big lazy circles.

✹ Adjust the elevator on the back edge of the wing to perfect the flight characteristics.

1.

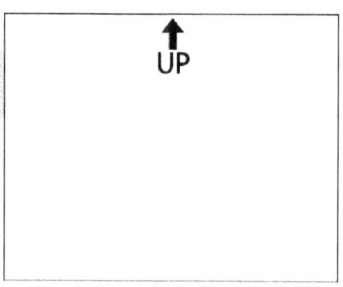

Orient the template so that the "UP" arrow is at the top of the page. Then flip the paper over so that none of the fold lines are showing.

2.

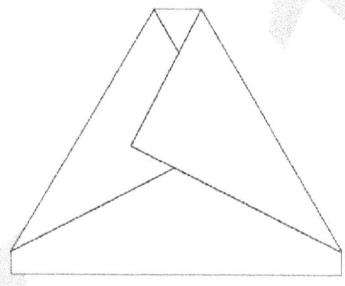

Fold the top right and top left corners in until fold lines 1 appear and crease along the dotted line.

RAPTOR

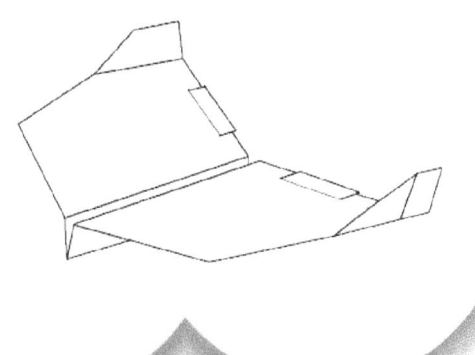

3.

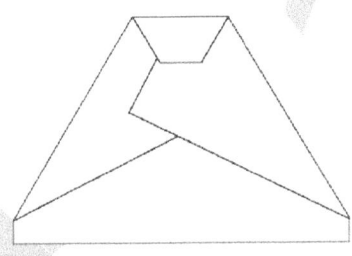

Fold the nose down toward you and crease along line 2.

4.

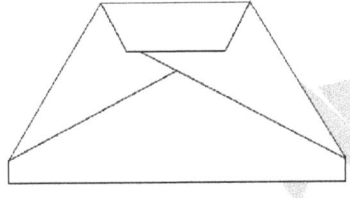

Fold the nose down toward you again and crease along fold line 3.

RAPTOR

5.

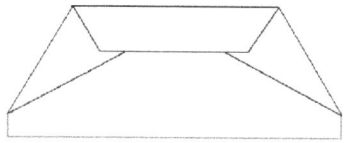

Fold the top edge down toward you again and crease along fold line 4.

6.

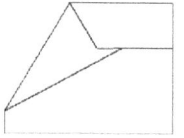

Flip the plane over and fold the right half over the left half along fold line 5.

RAPTOR

7.

Flip the wings down along fold lines 6 and the winglets up along fold lines 7. Cut slits along the back wing edge for the elevator adjustment. Add wing dihedral by tilting the wings up slightly away from the fuselage. The wings will have a slight "V" shape when viewed from the front. Happy flying!

DRAGONFLY

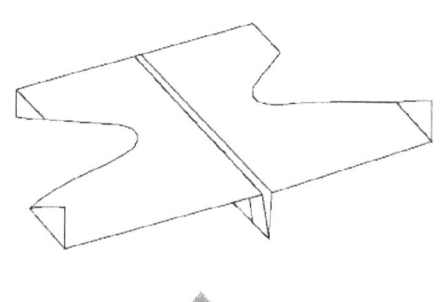

How it works:

✹ This unusual plane gets its name from its two sets of symmetrical wings that resemble a dragonfly when viewed from top.

✹ This plane is very aerobatic, and will tend to loop if thrown hard outdoors.

1.

Begin folding toward you along the first fold line. Continue folding this strip over itself until ou reach the stop line. Make firm creases with each fold.

2.

After you reach the stop line, flip your paper over and fold it in half fold line 2, so that the two flat sides of the paper are touching.

DRAGONFLY

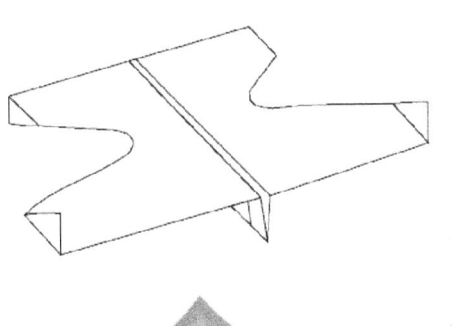

3.

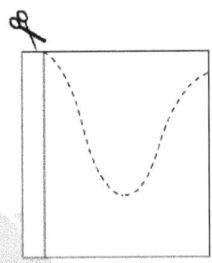

Cut along line 3 while keeping the paper folded tightly together to ensure that both wings match perfectly.

4.

Fold the wings down along fold line 4.

DRAGONFLY

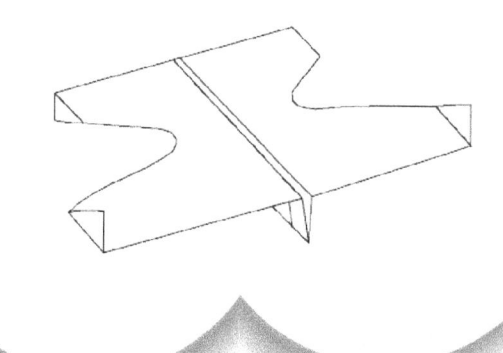

5. 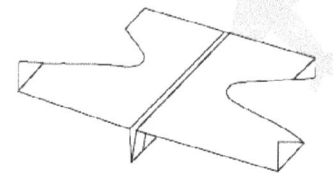 Fold the front winglets up along fold lines 5 and the back winglets down along fold lines 6. Add wing dihedral by tilting the wings up slightly away from the fuselage. The wings will have a slight "V" shape when viewed from the front. Happy flying!

BULLET

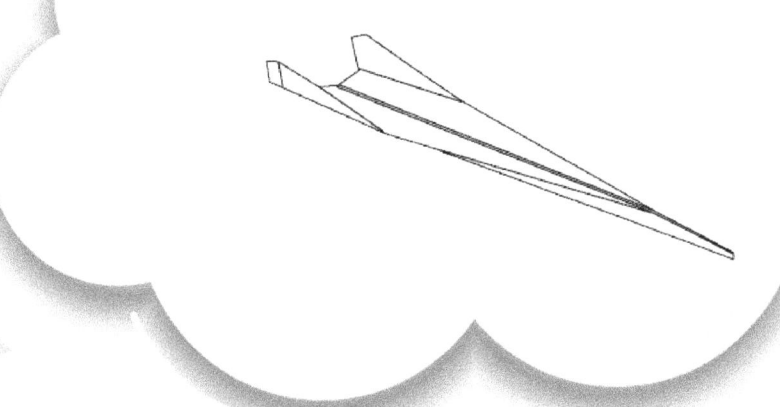

Tips:

✸ This plane flies as fast and as far as you can throw it, although it is not very stable during flight.

✸ It's a true dart and is very streamlined. The folds are very compact in this design, and accurate firm creases are critical.

1.

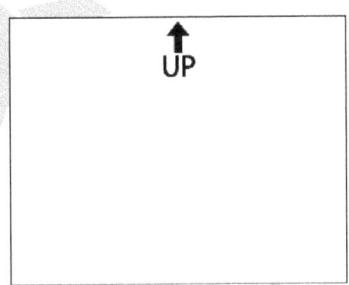

Orient the template so that the "UP" arrow is at the top of the page. Then flip the paper over so that none of the fold lines are showing.

2.

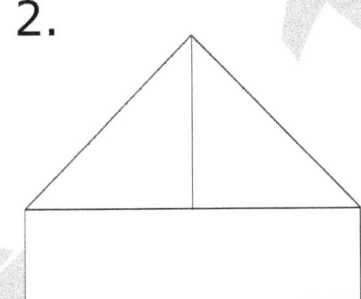

Fold the top left corner down toward you until fold line 1 becomes visible. Crease along the dotted line and repeat with the top right corner.

BULLET

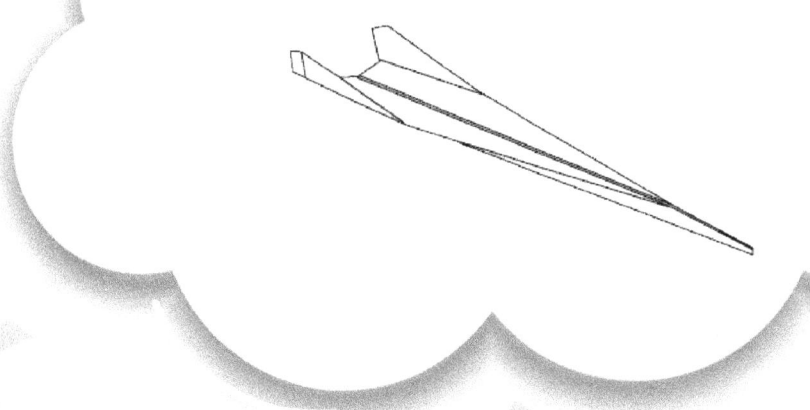

3.

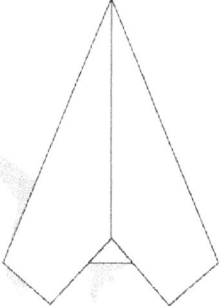

Fold the left side over again and crease along fold line 2. Repeat with the right side.

4.

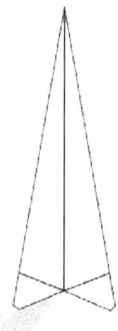

Fold the left side over once again and crease along fold line 3. Repeat with the right side. Make sure that you are making firm, crisp creases along each fold line.

BULLET

5.

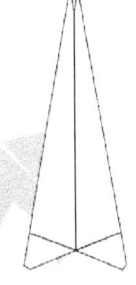

Fold the tip of the nose down toward you along the fold line.

6.

Fold the right half of the plane over onto the left half along fold line 4 so that the outside edges of the wings line up. Again, make a firm crease along this fold.

BULLET

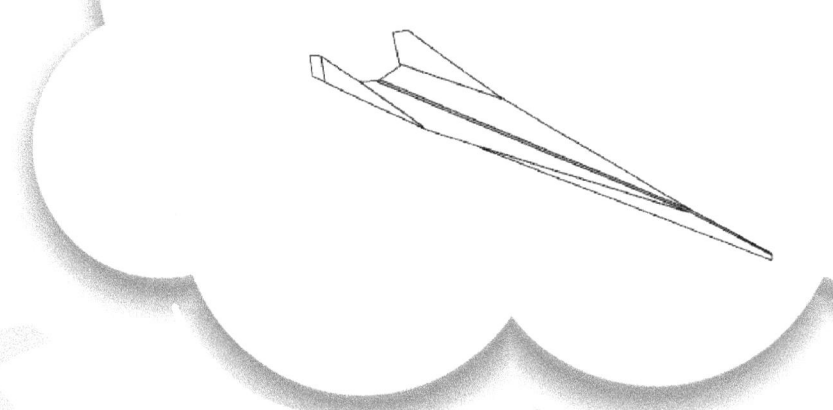

7.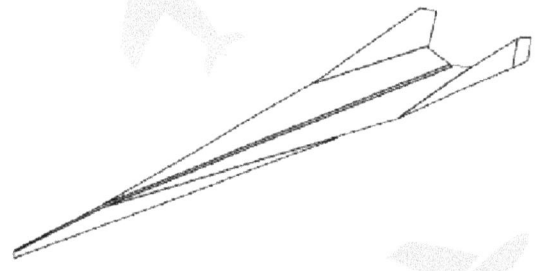

Fold the wings down along fold lines 5 and the winglets up along fold lines 6. Add wing dihedral by tilting the wings up slightly away from the fuselage. The wings will have a slight "V" shape when viewed from the front.
Happy flying!

INTERCEPTOR

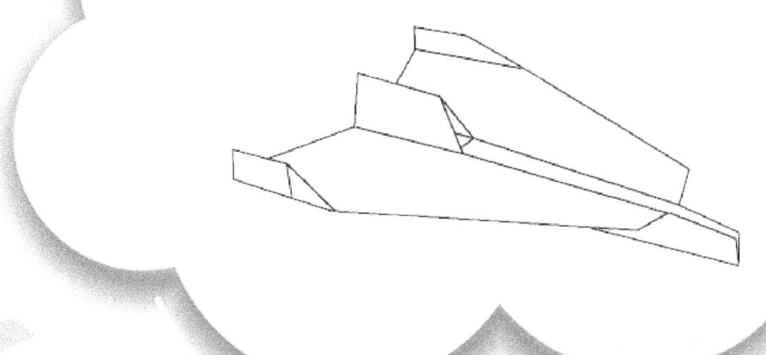

How it works:

✸ This plane has a central vertical stabilizer on the fuselage that help produce excellent straight flights.

✸ Make sure to complete the final step of the instructions for great performace.

1.

Orient the template with the "UP" arrow at the top of the page. Then, flip the paper over onto its backside, so that you cannot see any of the fold lines.

2.

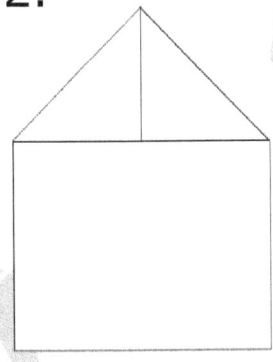

Pull the top right corner down toward you until fold line 1 is visible and crease along the dotted line. Repeat with the top left corner.

INTERCEPTOR

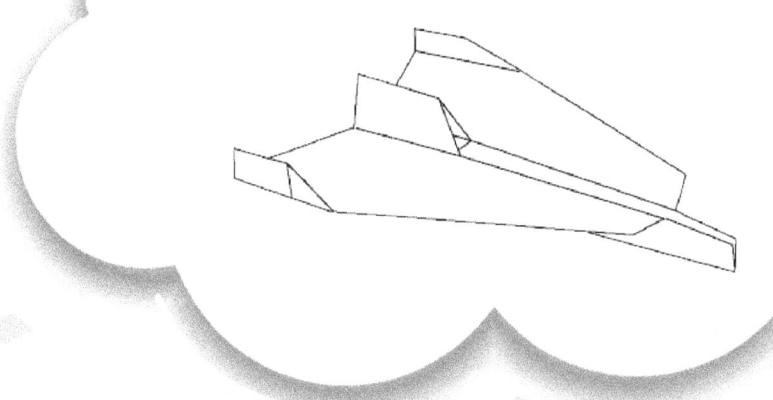

3.

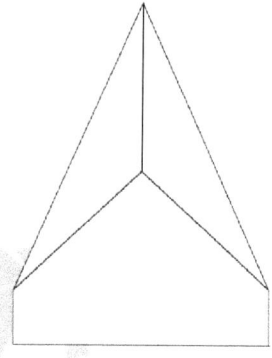

Fold the right side over again and crease along fold line 2. Repeat with the left side.

4.

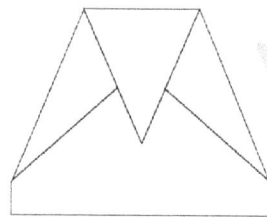

Fold the nose down toward you along fold line 3.

INTERCEPTOR

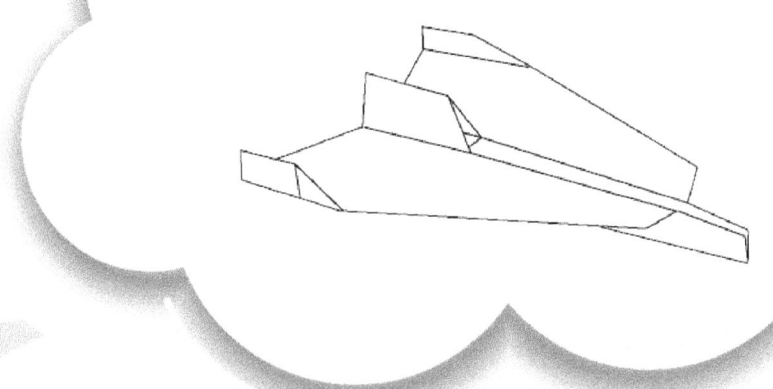

5.

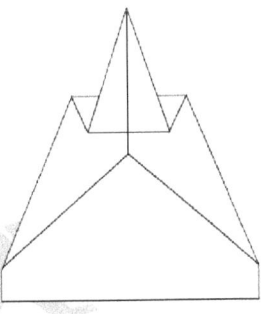

Fold the nose back up and crease along fold line 4.

6.

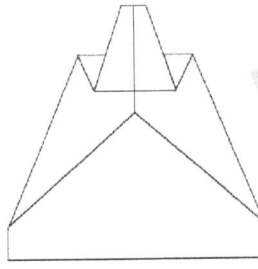

Fold the tip of the nose back away from you and crease along fold line 5.

INTERCEPTOR

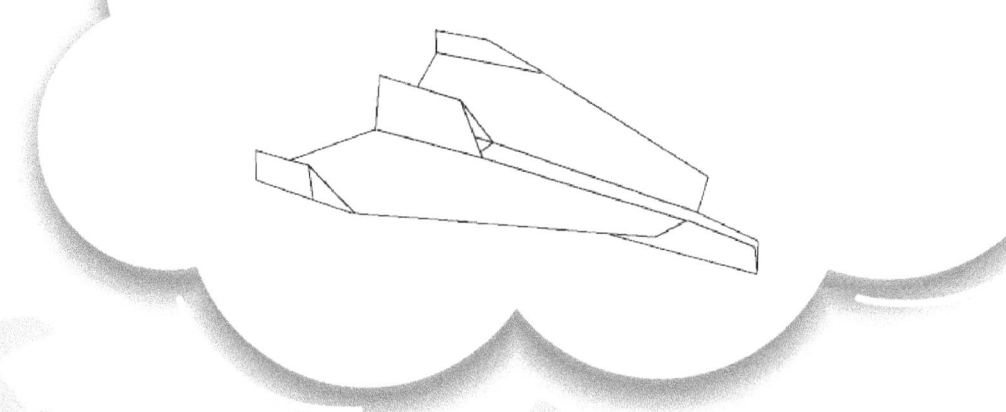

7.

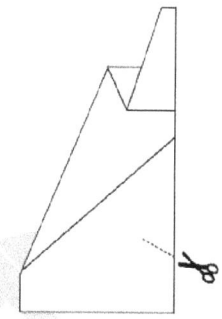

Flip the plane over. Fold the right half of the plane over onto the left half along fold line 6. Cut along the dotted line 7 for the vertical stabilizer.

8.

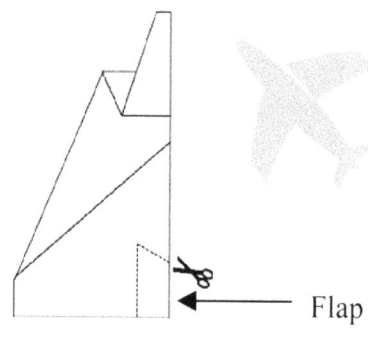

Flap

Tuck the flap that was formed by your cut between the two halves of the plane and crease it along fold line 8.

INTERCEPTOR

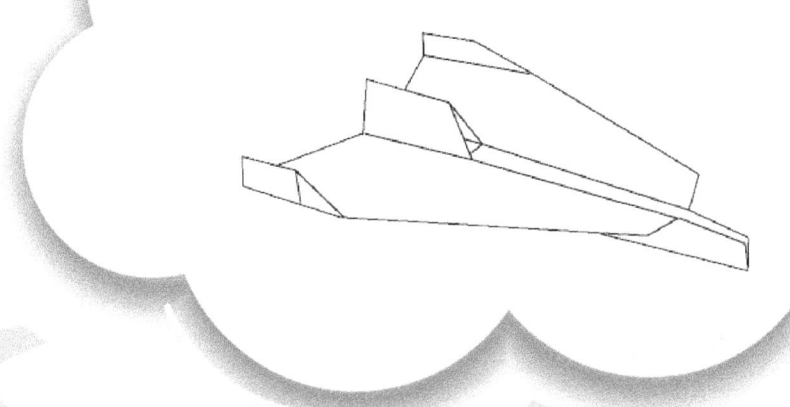

9.

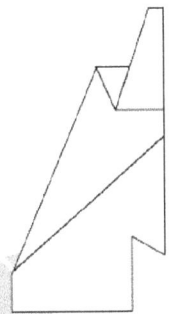

When you have completed the step above, your plane will look like this.

10.

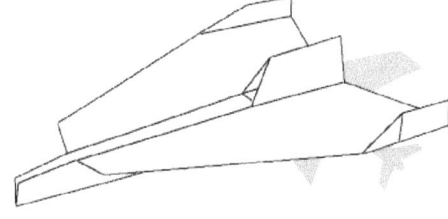

Fold the wings down along fold lines 8 and the winglets up along fold lines 9. Add wing dihedral by tilting the wings up slightly away from the fuselage. The wings will have a slight "V" shape when viewed from the front.

INTERCEPTOR

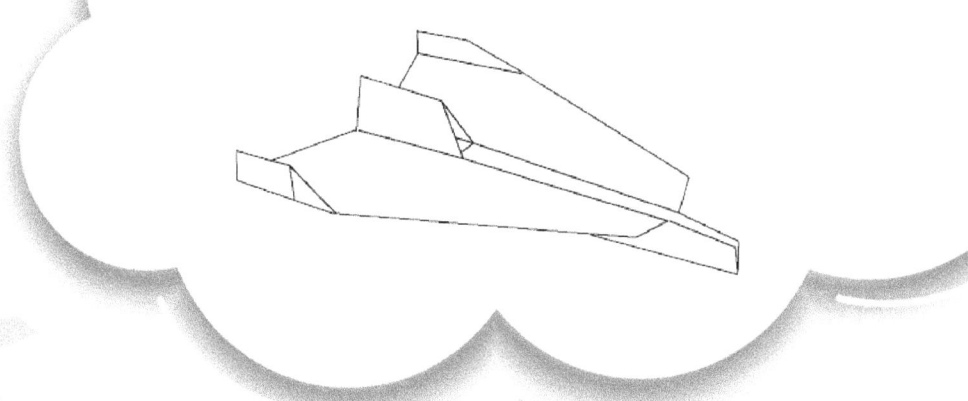

11.

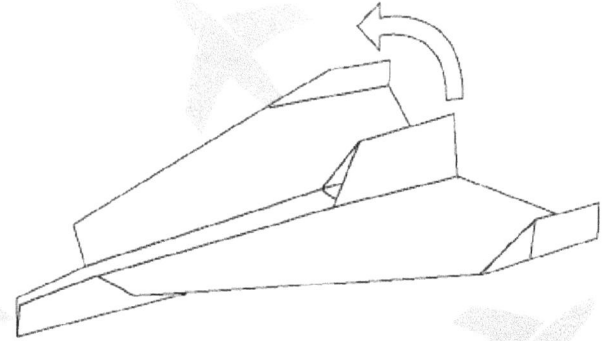

ATTENTION: Pull the back tip of the vertical stabilizer up and toward the front of the plane to put a slight upward curve to the trailing edge of the wings. This is to prevent the back edge of the wings from sagging downward. If you do not do this, your plane will nose-dive straight to the ground.
Happy flying!

STEALTH WING

Tips:

✸ This plane is an advanced design. With careful folding, it will reward you with long smooth glides.

✸ Launch gently from high above your head or an elevated area.

1.

Orient the template with the "UP" arrow at the top of the page. Then, flip the paper over onto its backside, so that you cannot see any of the fold lines.

2.

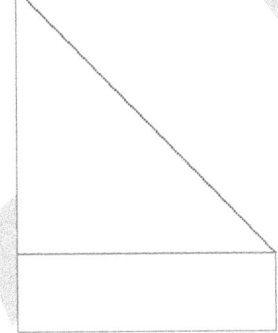

Fold the top right corner down and to the left until fold line 1 appears and crease along the dotted line.

STEALTH WING

3.

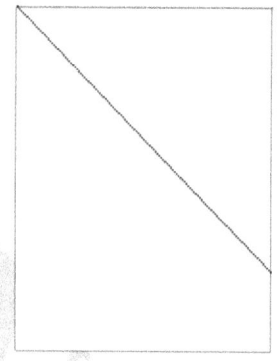

Unfold the fold you just created.

4.

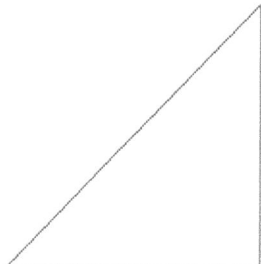

Repeat the procedure above by folding the top left corner down and to the right. Make a crease along fold line 2.

STEALTH WING

5.

Unfold the fold you just created.

6.

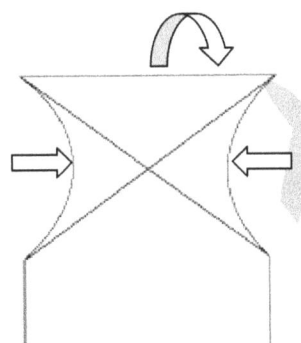

This step is a bit tricky. Lift the left and right edges of the paper and push them toward each other while folding the top triangle onto the bottom one. This will make a crease along the fold lines 3 so that you end up with the shape from the next page.

STEALTH WING

7.

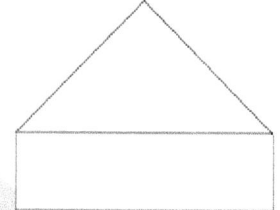

This is the shape you should have after completing the previous step.

8.

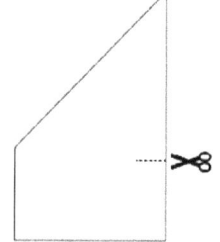

Fold the right side over onto the left side along fold line 4. Cut along the dotted cut line 5.

STEALTH WING

9.

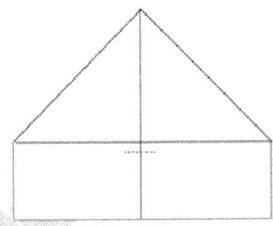

Unfold to produce this shape.

10.

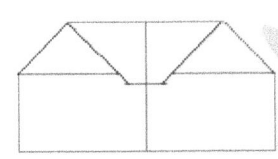

Fold the top point over and crease along fold line 6. Tuck the nose into the slit you cut along cut line 5.

STEALTH WING

11.

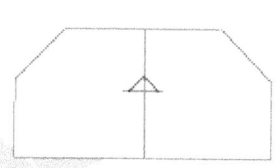

Flip the paper over and fold the nose up along fold line 7.

12.

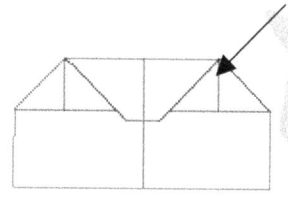

vertical fold line

Flip the paper back over again. Fold the top layer of the triangle shaped flaps in along the vertical fold line 8.

STEALTH WING

13.

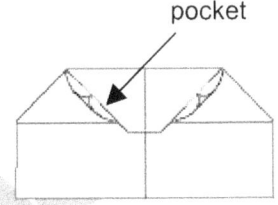

Tuck the flaps into the pockets near the nose of the plane. Push the flaps completely into the pockets.

14.

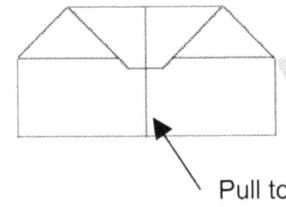

You should now see this shape. Locate the crease below cut line 5. Pull this crease toward you while also folding the plane in half toward you. This will create creases along fold lines 9.

STEALTH WING

15.

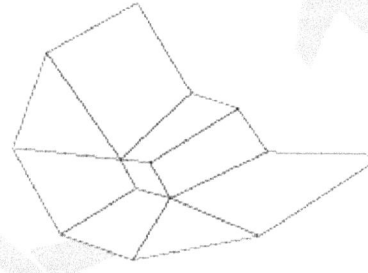

Partially unfold the fold you just created. You should see this shape.

16.

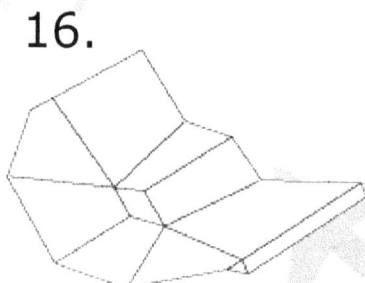

Fold down the winglets along fold lines 10. Now the plane is ready to fly! Hold the plane with your thumb against the nose and your index and middle finger behind cut line 5. Launch very gently from above your head.
Happy flying!

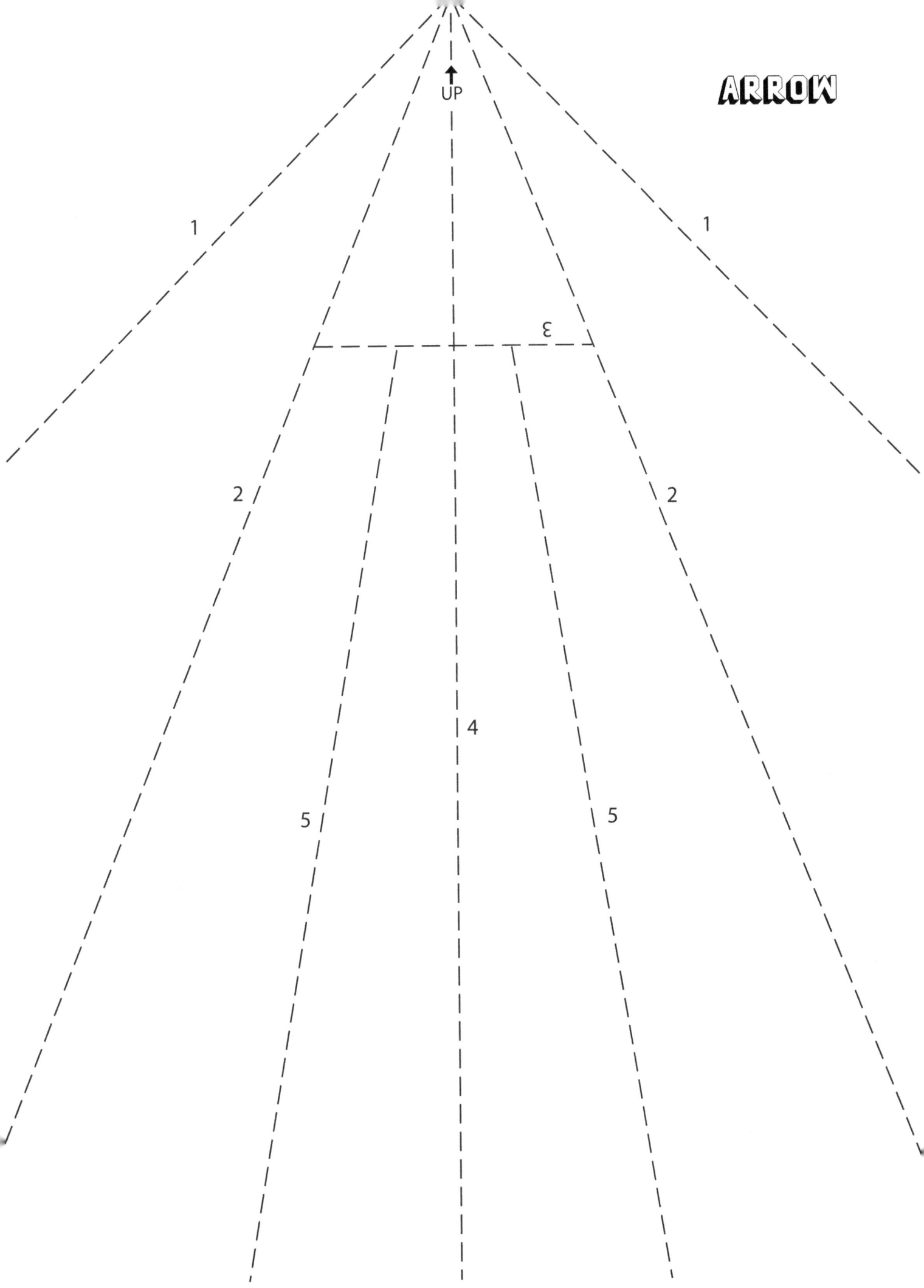

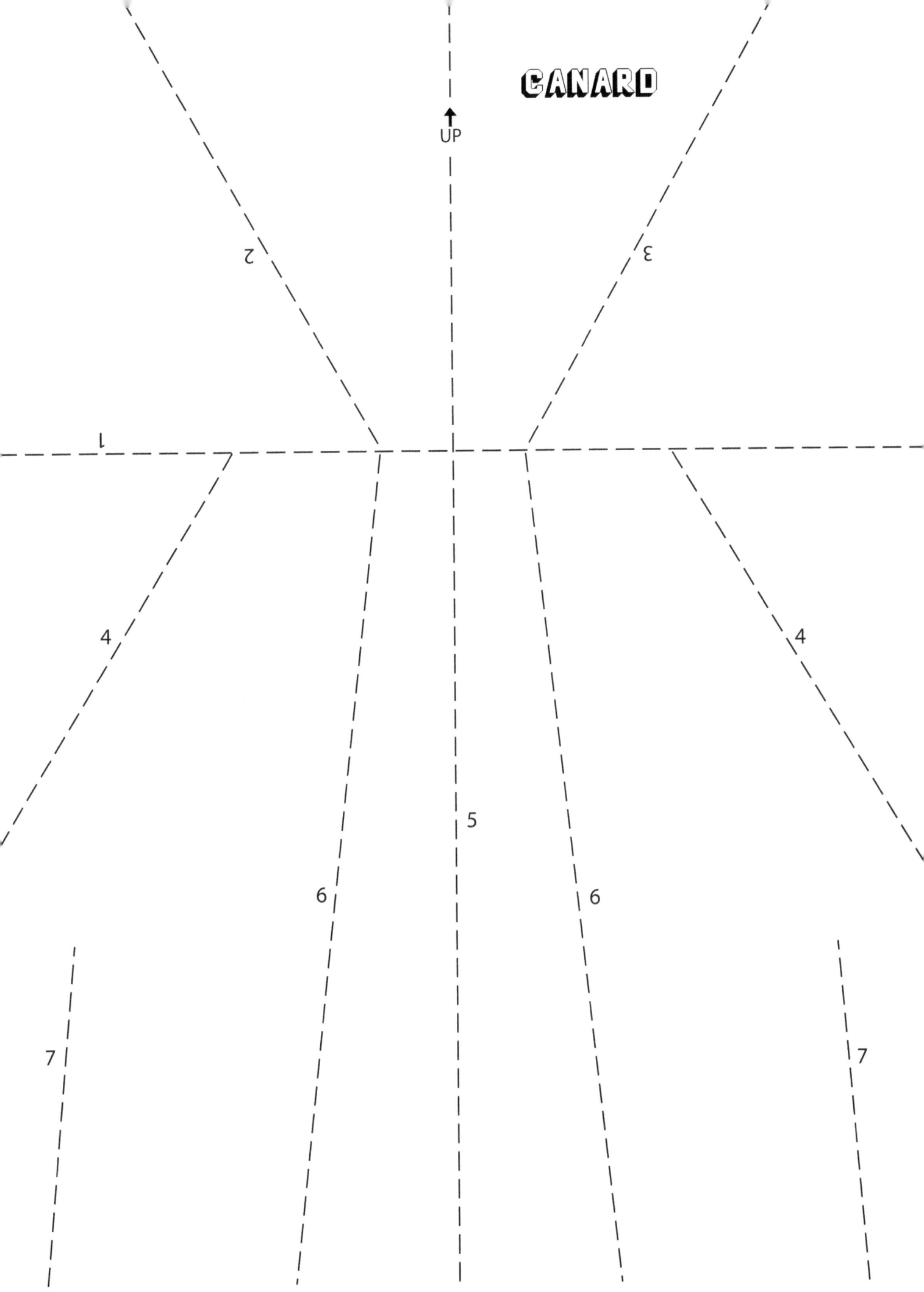

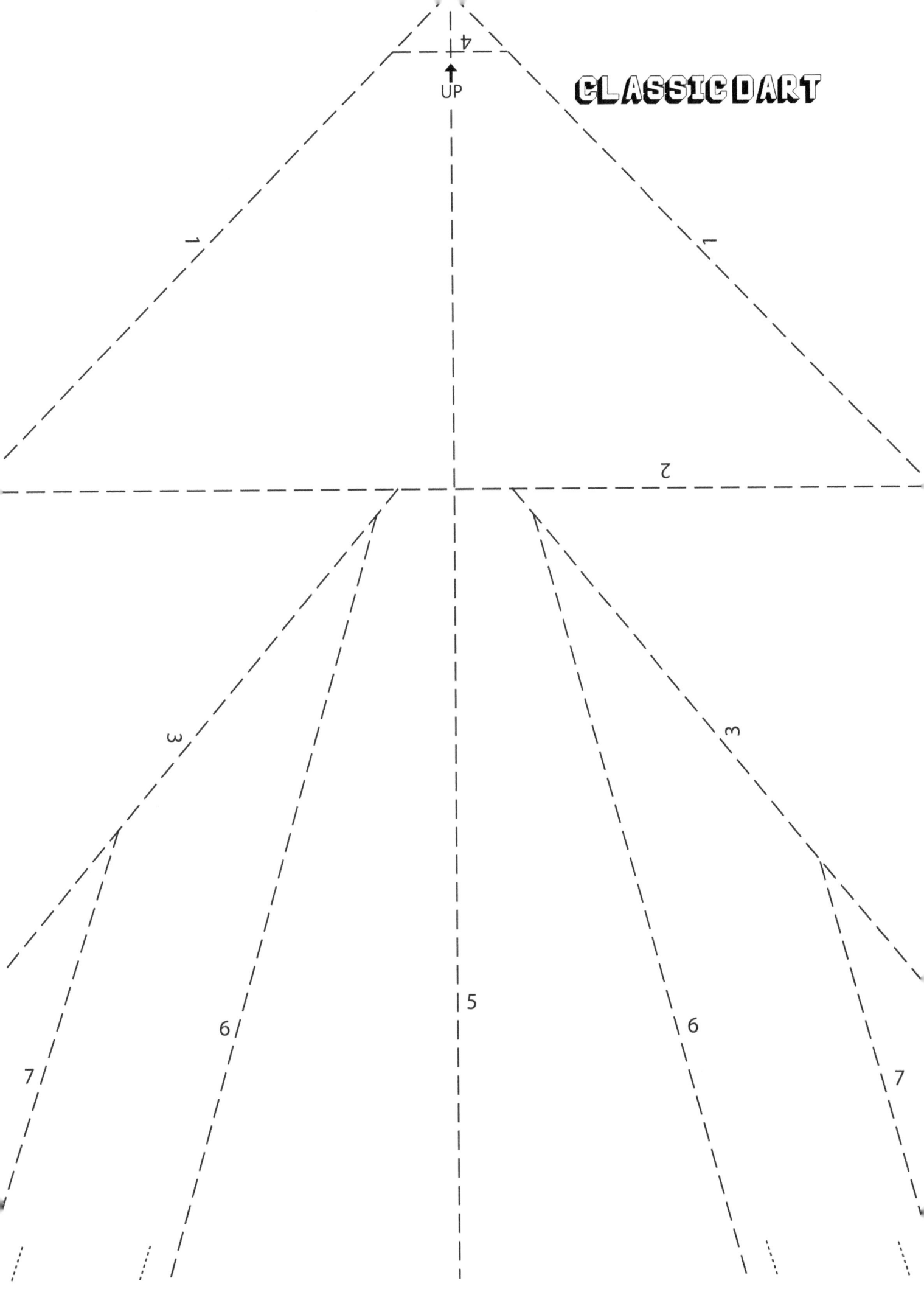

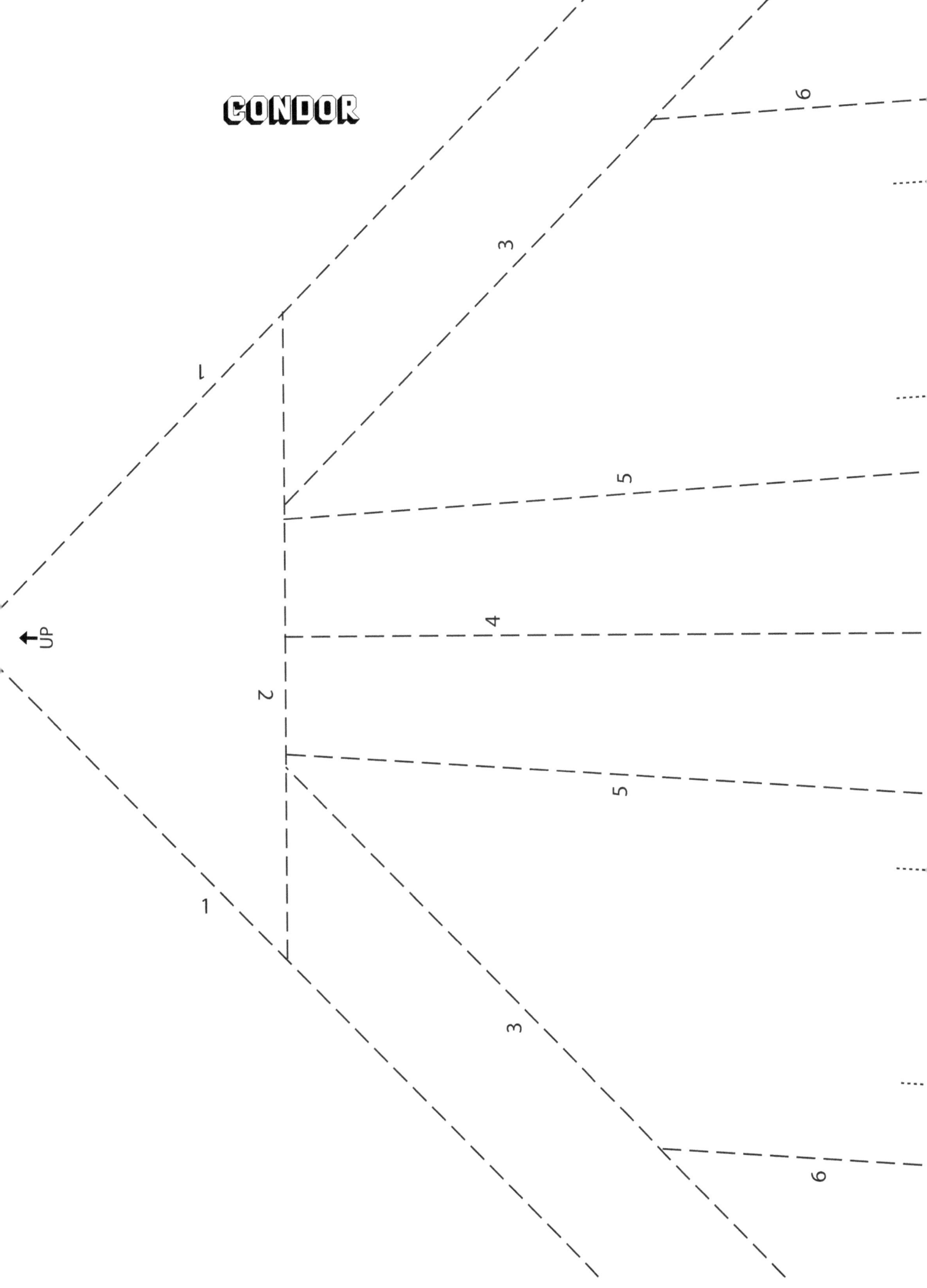

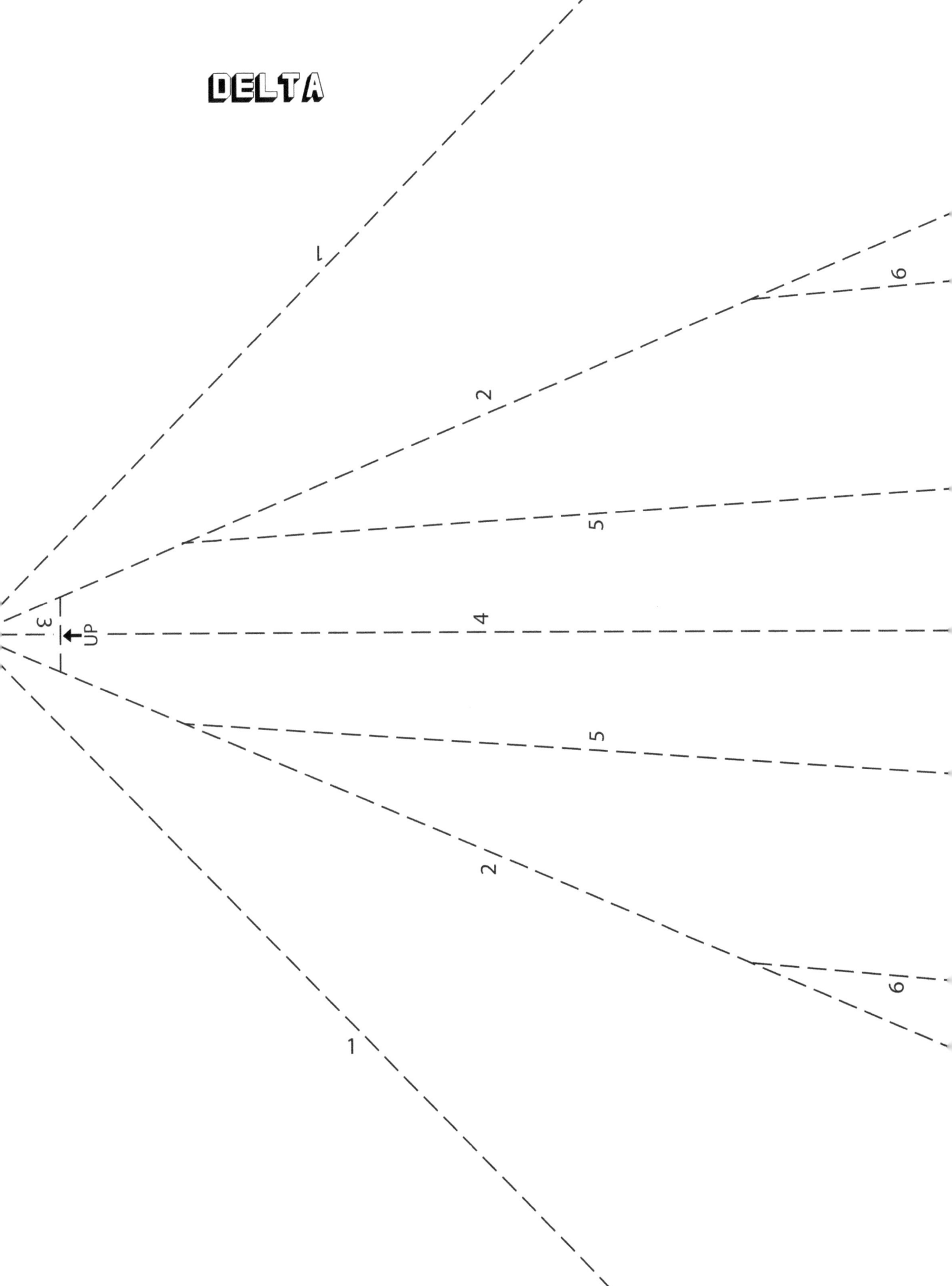

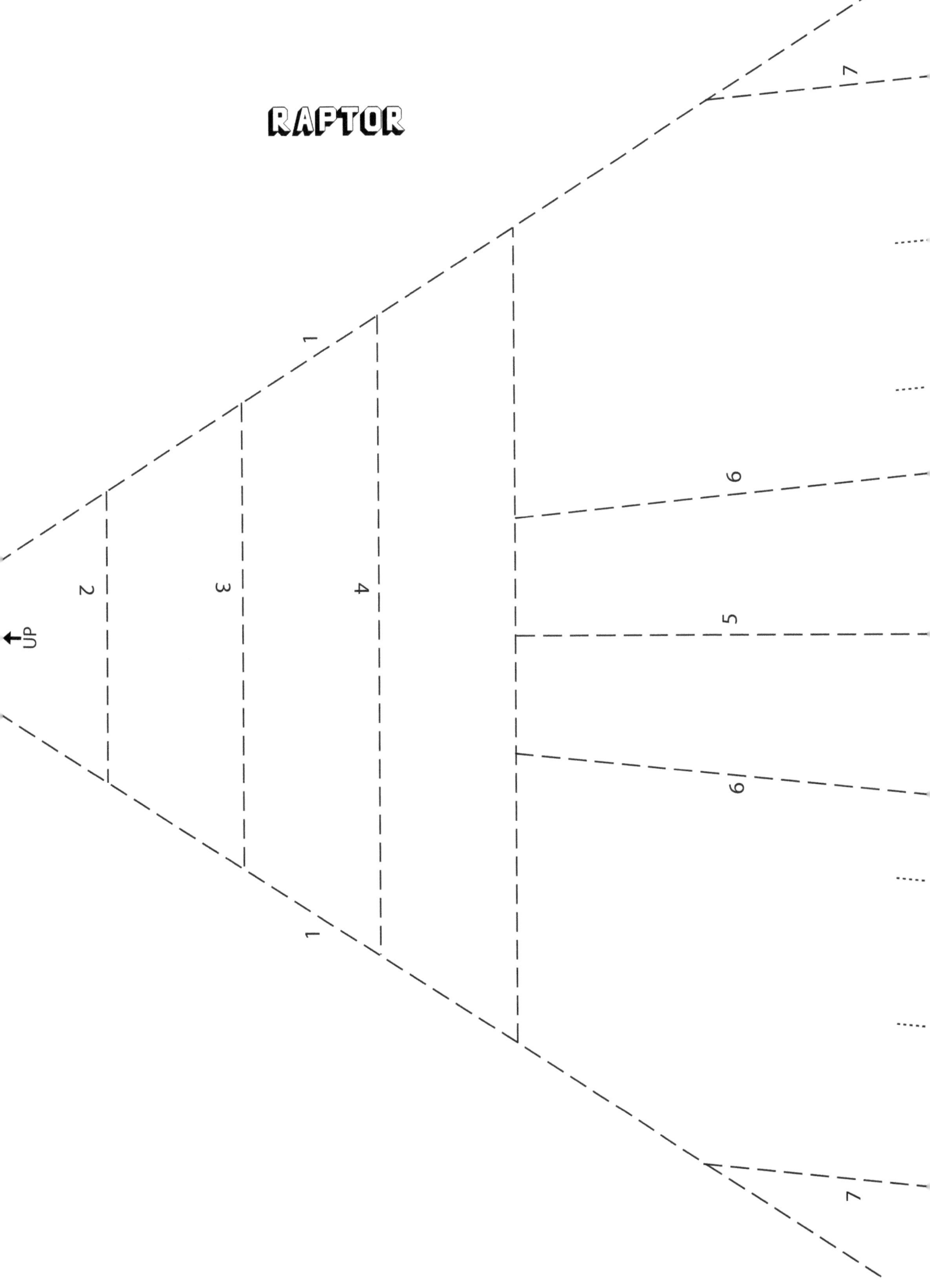

DRAGONFLY

MAKE FIRST FOLD ON THIS LINE — 1

STOP FOLDING WHEN YOU REACH THIS LINE — 2

4

3

5

6

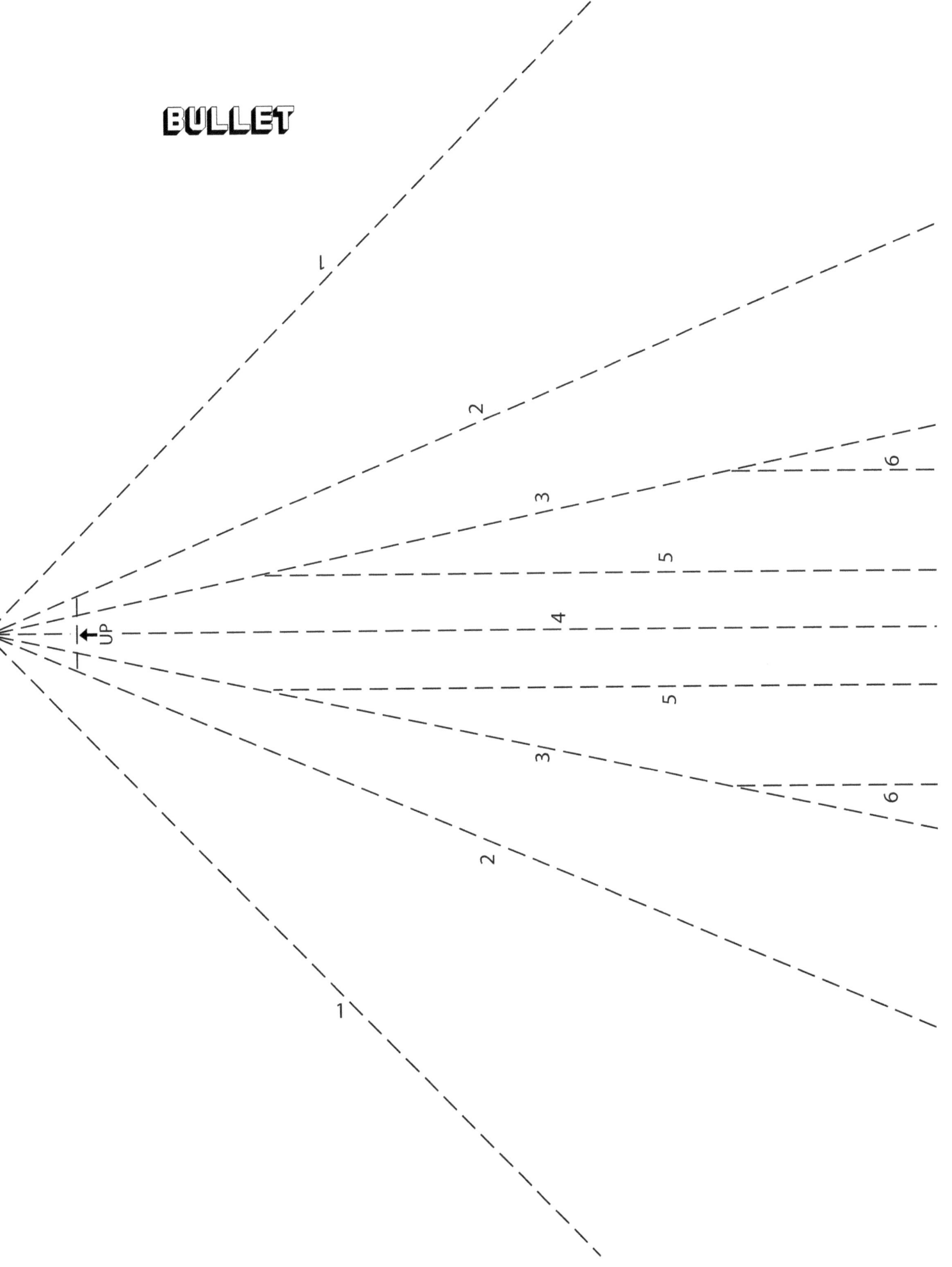

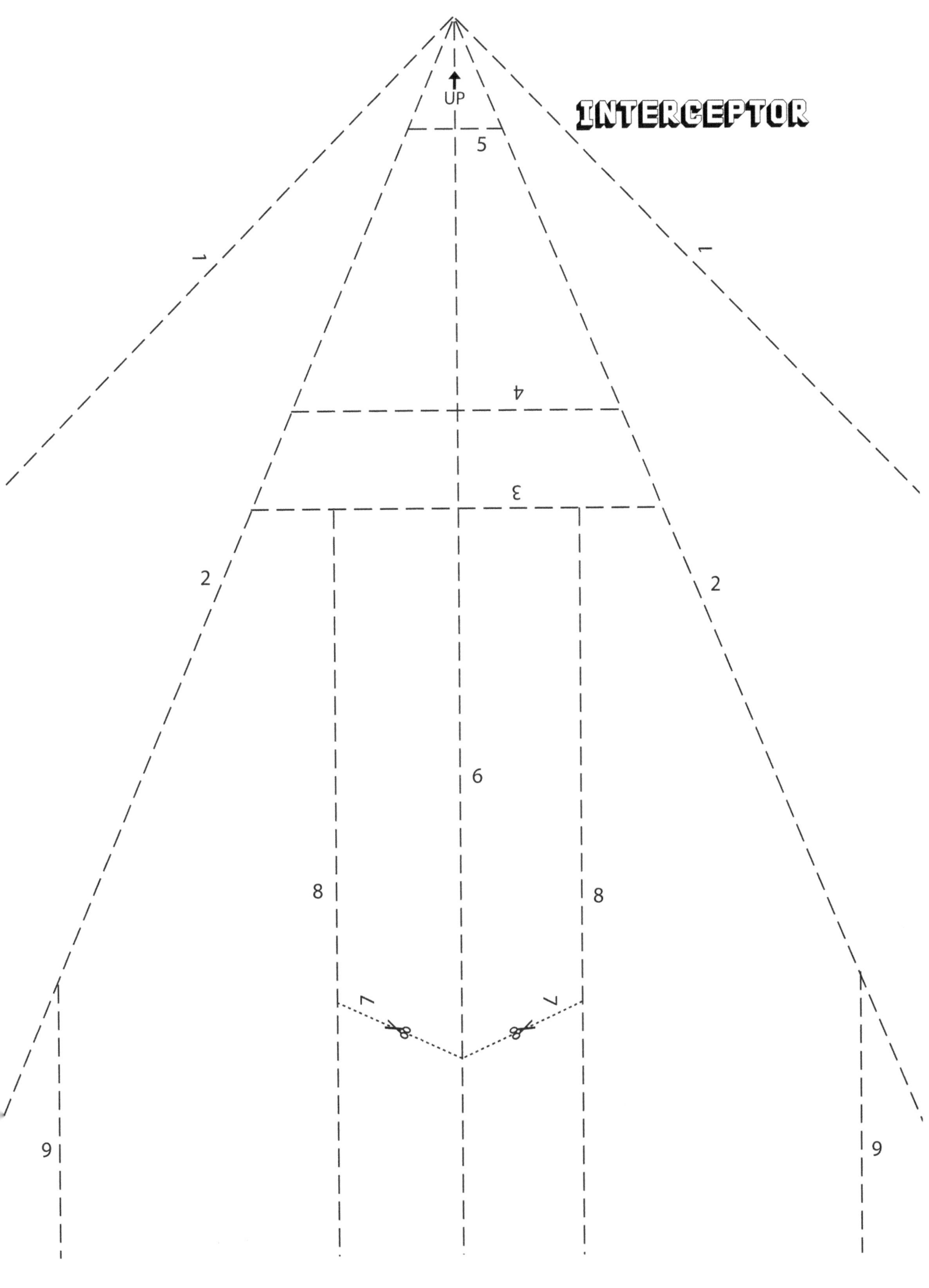

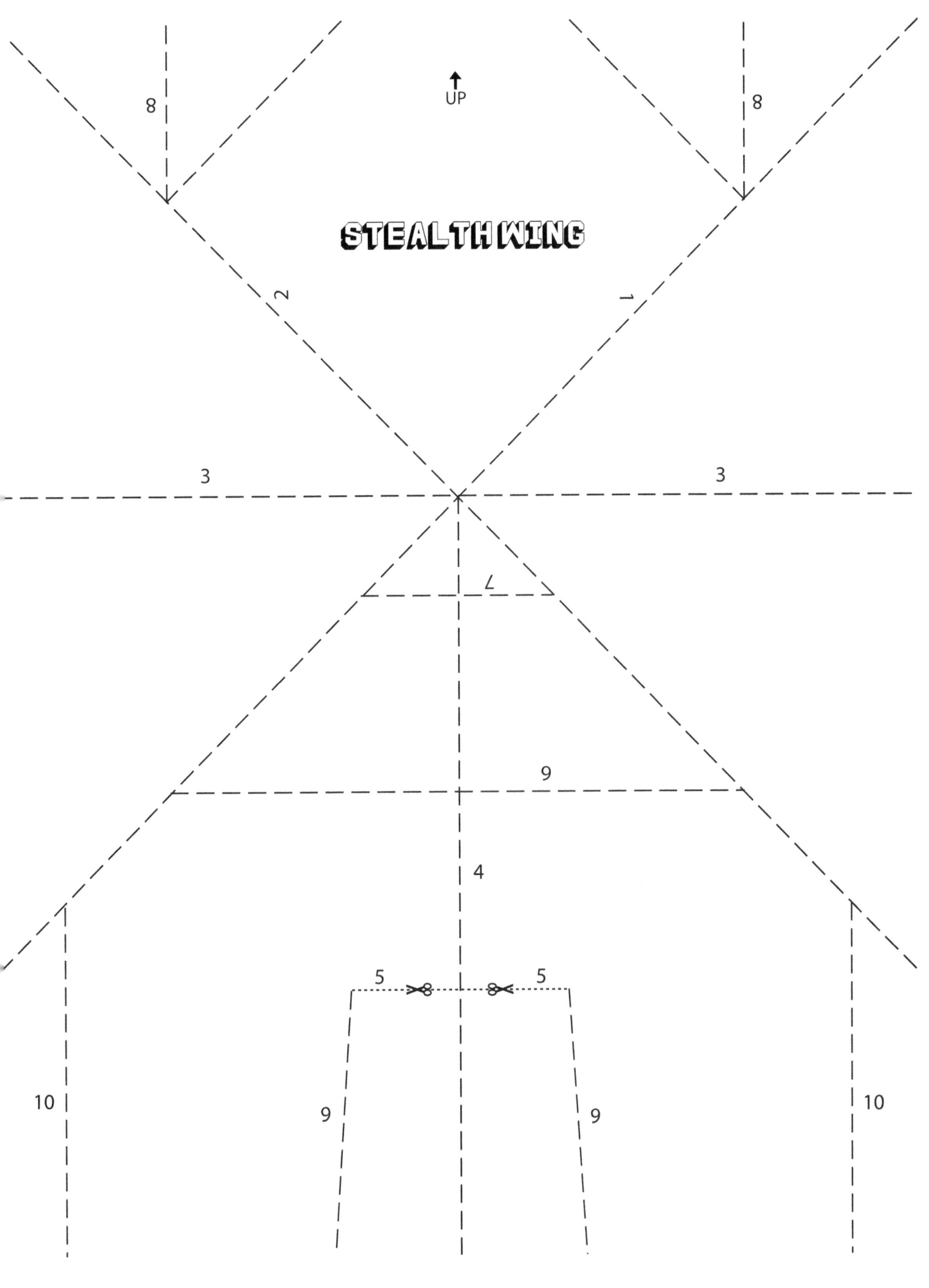

www.ingramcontent.com/pod-product-compliance
Ingram Content Group UK Ltd.
Pitfield, Milton Keynes, MK11 3LW, UK
UKHW050415240426
12048UKWH00020B/1515

9 783755 102854